T0167057

Where will I live
NOW?

Where will I live
NOW?

*Knowing more about senior housing choices
will have a positive impact on your life.*

J. Anthony Burke

iUniverse LLC
Bloomington

Where will I live NOW?
Knowing more about senior housing choices
will have a positive impact on your life.

iUniverse books may be ordered through booksellers or by contacting:

iUniverse LLC
1663 Liberty Drive
Bloomington, IN 47403
www.iuniverse.com
1-800-Authors (1-800-288-4677)

ISBN: 978-1-4917-0583-4 (sc)
ISBN: 978-1-4917-0584-1 (ebk)

Printed in the United States of America

iUniverse rev. date: 09/04/2013

Contents

Special Thanks

When I first published this book in 2001, my wife and I spent what seemed to be every waking moment gathering information, visiting senior residents of assisted living homes, talking with family, friends, doctors, nurses and others in an effort to find a suitable living accommodation for my wife's mother.

I want to acknowledge in this book how very exceptional my wife and family were throughout the entire time we were involved in trying to understand what her mother needed in terms of extra care and during our search for that care.

I also want to say that my wife remained very strong during that trying time of caring for her mother, working with me to find proper assistance for her and holding down a full time job. I learned a great deal from her about patience and how important it was to work as a family to accomplish the daunting task ahead of us.

Since then, we have become very familiar with senior living accommodations, what they each offer and don't offer, and I wanted to chronicle our journey in an updated book. Since then, I have become a "boomer and senior advocate," working to help people in this stage of their lives to live a better more satisfying life.

I initially wrote this book to share the experiences we had helping my mother-in-law move from an independent lifestyle into an assisted living facility.

Since that time, my parents moved into a Continuing Care Retirement Community (CCRC) and my mother has since transferred to a nursing home.

I will discuss these and other living accommodation options in this book. Hopefully this book will serve as a resource so that you will have as much information as possible to help you evaluate all of your housing choices and make good decisions.

I hope I can give you some useful suggestions and help, in the event you also are faced with the task and challenge of searching for a new living accommodation for yourself or an aging senior. I want to warn you that this journey will not be easy, because it is much more than "just another move" as you will read in the following pages.

What makes this move so challenging is that it usually occurs when your senior's health has deteriorated to the point he or she is no longer able to live alone. This experience becomes supercharged with every emotion imaginable. However, if you follow the suggestions in this book, you will get thorough it, hopefully with less pain and angst and you will find a new living arrangement that is suitable to you and your loved one.

J. Anthony Burke

I.   *Introduction*

My wife and I lived in a wonderful community in Howard County, Maryland for over 30 years. We raised three fabulous children and even moved my wife's mother, who was a widow at the time of my first book, to our community so that she could be close to us yet still live independently.

She moved into a mid-rise apartment complex for seniors at the time and enjoyed a terrific, active, independent life. She was able to be close to her daughter when she wanted, spend time with her friends when she wanted and we were able to be with her frequently to see that she was doing well.

Life was good for a number of years, but changed dramatically for all of us in a matter of days. My mother-in-law was in her late eighties at the time and became ill with bronchitis (nearly pneumonia) and had to be hospitalized for a couple of days.

Once hospitalized, her life and our lives were never quite the same. Her needs changed significantly. Up to that point she had been a healthy, happy, active 87-year-old woman who loved life, her family and friends.

After the hospital stay, she moved back to her apartment, but it became very apparent to me and my wife that her mother could not continue to live independently as she had for many years. It was, however, not that apparent to my mother-in-law.

She believed, and tried very hard to convince all of us that she would bounce back and deep down inside we wanted to believe it too.

Unfortunately we could see that progress was slow and phone calls to us at all hours of the day and night became more frequent. These were calls for help in one way or another and of course we reacted with care and love to assist her.

My wife and I realized after a few weeks of giving nearly daily assistance to her mother that we needed help for our own well-being and hers and that it may be time to seek some assistance for her.

She could still get around her apartment using a walker or cane but it was painful to watch her move in baby steps to get to the bathroom on her own.

We thoughtfully began the arduous task of investigating new living accommodations for my wife's mother (a path we later followed with my mother) and learned a great deal in the process.

I wrote this book to offer some help and guidance to you, boomers like us, who are facing the same or similar circumstances with an aging, senior loved one.

Caring for an aging senior is not an easy situation, to which my wife and I can attest, but with planning, time, the right information and thoughtful questions you will get through it.

As a result, you and your loved one, who needs assistance, will live a better, happier life. We wish you all the best in you search for a new living accommodation for you and or your senior and hope this information helps in some small way.

If your senior ever asks that dreaded question, 'Where will I live now' you will have some answers.

II. "Boomers like us"

I am reaching out to other boomers like us to create a forum for information sharing, a place in which boomers and seniors can learn from and assist each other and improve the quality of each of our lives. I am doing this through social media on the Web.

I publish a blog, www.boomerandseniornews.wordpress.com, where I write about issues relevant to boomers and seniors and I would appreciate receiving your comments. What is important to you in your life? What help do you need? What experiences have you had that can help others?

I suggest that most boomers would like to know about your experiences and how you managed through them. I consider this a self-help site *"for and about boomers and seniors."* If you were born in the United States between 1946 and 1964 then you are a member of this fabulous community.

According to a report on CBS about 78 million baby boomers are living in the United States today and 65.1 million of them are online. They spend 40 hours a month online and control 70 percent of the wealth in the U.S.*. In fact, they account for one third (the largest constituency) of the 195.3 million Internet users in the U.S.

We consider ourselves typical American, middle class "boomers", who have three wonderful, adult children and we are proud grandparents. I have worked for many years in the media business and wow has that changed dramatically with the advent of the Internet!

My wife worked for the Federal Government for the first few years of marriage then became a stay-at-home mom until the children started high school and then entered the work force again at a pediatric practice.

My wife and I have worked hard our entire lives, as you have, to provide an education, a good safe home life and sound guidance for our children. We have tried to put money away for our future so that we don't end up impoverished and have to rely entirely on the state and or our children for support.

We were care givers for my wife's mother and are current caregivers along with my sister for my mother, who lives in a nursing home. We have great concerns that life for boomers is changing dramatically especially considering the great recession of 2008 and that as we enter another stage in our lives, seemingly with greater responsibilities and many more pressures we don't want to be forgotten or ignored.

By this we mean ignored by local, state and federal government, health insurance providers, drug companies, employers, businesses in general, and society in general.

We are a powerful community of 78 million boomers, who should and could be talking with each other more, sharing needed information that affects us all, letting our elected representatives know what is in our best collective interest and working harder for each other.

The Internet can help make all of this possible. It is a fabulous technology and can be a powerful information-sharing conduit for boomers like us.

Sources:
*Engage: Boomers blog Monday, May 20, 2013

Again, I would like you to think of my blog as a community *"for and about boomers and seniors"* on which you can comment about a variety of topics, including, but not limited to, general health, living a healthy lifestyle, staying fit, reviewing products and services that affect boomers, reviewing drugs designed for boomers, reviewing and commenting on the ever-rising cost of health care.

We would like to have you share your experiences on all of the following topics to illustrate or make points. You can write and comment about Social Security, Medicare, Medicaid, how and what you think Congress is doing on your behalf.

Other topics might be caring for your parents, putting your children through college, grand-parenting, discussing retirement living choices for boomers.

You may want to discuss selling your home, reviewing and referring home service contractors and other service providers in your area whom you think are exceptional. You may want to refer employment opportunities for boomers, discuss financial topics for boomers, elder law topics and so much more.

The goal is to develop a very large community of interested, concerned boomers. The only thing we ask is that when you write and comment on the site that you be respectful of others and not use objectionable language. Thanks very much and we look forward to sharing with you.

<u>Boomers are in a tough spot</u>

Boomers have become known as the "*sandwich generation*", with children for whom we may still be caring on one end and our parents who need special care and assistance, on the other. The following are some highlights of a study conducted by Communispace on the topic of "The sandwich generation".

Role Reversal

According to a recent study by Communispace, "the recession has added considerable stress to this already overburdened population known as 'the sandwich generation,' baby boomers who support kids, parents, relatives and themselves at the same time.

A significant finding is that this caretaker segment is more of a "situation" than a generation. It includes people ranging from their mid-30s to 60 and over who will sacrifice more for their parents, even if it's at the expense of their children:

- 58% said they'd give a spare bedroom to an aging parent over their young adult child
- 65% said they'd move in with an ailing parent, even if it meant a longer commute and new environment (school, friends, etc) for their child or children
- 77% would adapt the things they'd purchase to accommodate parents; for example, when buying a new car they'd consider buying one with a larger trunk (to hold a parent's wheel chair or walker), rather than one that is comfortable or gets good gas mileage".

According to the Pew Research Center, 47 percent of adults in their 40s and 50s belong to the sandwich generation. The population has grown so large that the month of July 2013 was dedicated to raising awareness about the Sandwich Generation.

Source: An Excerpt from the Center for Media Research, Wednesday, October 21, 2009

Some Boomer Statistics:

For those of you who are interested in quantifying the boomer generation further, below are some boomer demographic statistics: This should provide you with the sense that boomers are a powerful segment of American society today.

78 million Americans who were 50 or older as of 2001, now control 70% of the country's wealth. (U.S. Census and Federal Reserve).

- 85% of boomers see their retirement as a time for "learning and self-discovery", 65% for "reinventing oneself" and 51% for a "new beginning." About nine in 10 (88%) see it as a new phase of personal growth and development. Also, six in 10 say they plan to work because they want to, not because they have to. (According to the survey by American Express Financial Advisors).

- Two thirds of Americans ages 50-64 use the Internet. (Pew Internet & American Life Project)

- Households headed by someone in the 55-to-64 age group had a median net worth of $112,048 in 2000-15 times the $7,240 reported for the under-35-age group. Within five years about a third of the population is going to be at least 50 years old. (U.S. Census and Federal Reserve).

- The 50+ have $2.4 trillion in annual income, which accounts for 42% of all after-tax income. This Includes banking accounts, securities, etc.

(U.S. Consumer Expenditure Survey).

More Boomer Statistics

- Adults 50 and older accounted for an estimated $1 trillion+ in total expenditures in 2005. (U.S. Consumer Expenditure Survey and FINDSVP projection).

- The life expectancy for people who live to age 65 is an additional 18 years, or to age 83*)*. The life expectancy for those who live to age 65 is higher for women, almost 20 years, than for men, almost 17 years. (According to the *National Center for Health Statistics)*

- 78 million people were born between 1946 and 1964. (NCPA Idea House)

- The first baby boomer turned 60 on January 1, 2006.

- Currently, there are more than 40,000 centenarians in the United States, or a little more than one centenarian per 10,000 in the populations; 85% of them are women, 15% are men.

(Dr. Thomas Perls, Boston University School of Medicine, New England Centenarians Study).

Sources:

U.S.Census and Federal Reserve

U.S. Consumer Expenditure Survey and FINDSVP projection

U.S. Consumer Expenditure Survey

Pew Internet & American Life Project
Survey by American Express Financial Advisors
\National Center for Health Statistics
NCPA Idea House

III.   Determining your
(The Boomer's) needs

If you are a boomer or senior who is considering a move to a new living accommodation, because you had a life changing event, such as divorce or death of a spouse or just want to downsize and get rid of all of the work you anticipate having to do on the house, you have many choices available today compared to 10 or 20 years ago.

There is often an issue of a lowering of income due to a major life event such as a death of a spouse which means you don't want the expense of maintaining your large, single family home any longer. If you are a boomer or senior who is facing a divorce you may need to make a move to a more affordable housing accommodation.

For a more affordable housing accommodation you may want to consider senior apartment housing, which falls into a few categories such as luxury, market rate and affordable. Given a tight budget it may make sense for you to move to an affordable senior apartment in your area that has your desired benefits and amenities.

The amount you will spend on a senior apartment will be far less than what you are used to shelling out for your single family home considering the upkeep and maintenance. Affordable housing is in demand today and unfortunately in short supply due to significant demographic changes over the past few years.

An affordable senior apartment will generally allow you to spend no more than 30% of your income on rent and utilities. There are however some senior apartments that offer luxury amenities such as on-site restaurants, exercise facilities, transportation, walking trails, even a nurse on-site. These services and amenities have a price tag, but compared to what you have been paying to keep up your house it could seem like a bargain. I encourage you to visit several senior apartments in your area to find the one that best meets your needs.

If you have the financial resources and are in fairly good health and don't believe you need much assistance at this point with daily living activities, then you may want to consider some housing choices other than ones described above or in chapter V.

There are a number of housing alternatives available to boomers and seniors who have relatively good health and the necessary resources that are seeing a growth trend compared to a 10 or more years ago.

55+ Active Adult Communities

One of them is the 55+ Active Adult Lifestyle Community. My wife and I got serious a couple of years ago about moving to a more carefree home and lifestyle. While we were still working and not interested in retiring at the time, we were interested in not having to do daily yard maintenance and snow removal any longer. We had been in our single family house on a heavily treed lot for over 30 years and spent much of our free time working in the yard and or maintaining the house to make sure when it was time to move, we didn't have to scramble to get it ready.

We searched for a few months for the right 55+ community that had the right amount of amenities, was affordable and was still close enough to our children. We finally decided to move into an active adult community in the winter of 2010 and found it to be exactly what we wanted.

There are literally thousands of 55+ Active Adult Communities across the United States being built by some of the best know national home builders and each has some unique characteristics. Some are luxury communities, others feature a golf course and yet others have a pool, club house with exercise rooms, entertainment areas and tennis courts to encourage residents to be as active as they want. Most communities also encourage their residents to become active in clubs of interest and committees that serve the residents at large. We have found there is always something to do in our community.

In some 55+ communities you can rent your home so you can experience the lifestyle before you buy. In others you have to buy the house and agree not to buy for investment and rent out at least in the first couple of years. There are communities with condominium ownership and still others where you can purchase in fee simple ownership.

The choices are numerous but they all have certain characteristics in common. First and foremost, one person in the house must be at least 55 years old in order to take ownership of a home and there are fairly strict rules about any children living in the house who are under 19 years old. Grandchildren under 19 years old in many communities are allowed to visit overnight, but with a maximum number of nights allowed in a month or quarter. Violating these rules will invite the scrutiny of the community's board of directors and there could be penalties so you will need to pay close attention to these restrictions.

55+ Active adult communities offer better design options today and the homes are much better built than 10 or more years ago. They are more comfortable, easier and safer with security systems built into the homes and some are in secure, gated communities. Active adult communities are built to encourage independent living and are built with livable designs in mind. Chief among the livable design elements are master suites on the first floor and interior doors wide enough for wheelchairs if needed. Master bathrooms are built with higher toilets than normal making it much easier for the boomer or senior who has difficulty with traditional low toilets. These are design elements that are built-in knowing they will be appreciated and valued by the boomer and senior demographic.

All 55+ communities offer the residents an opportunity to live a more carefree lifestyle where the HOA handles the mundane, but sometimes back-breaking chores such as landscaping, grass cutting, mulching, pruning, leaf raking and snow removal in colder climate communities, just the things you are trying to avoid at this phase in your life.

Of course there is a monthly HOA fee each residential unit pays for these services and they vary greatly depending on the location, depth of services and amenities. Make sure to ask the community salesperson to provide you with a complete list of services and read them carefully before you sign the contract to purchase. Nobody likes surprises especially when you are about to invest a significant amount of money in a new house.

If you decide to move to a 55+ active adult community, either condominium ownership or fee simple ownership, there are often strict covenants to which you have to agree before you can purchase there. As an example, when you want to alter anything on the outside of your house or property you will need to fill out an architectural alteration form for the architectural committee to review and either approve or deny based on alteration policies in the covenants.

Keep in mind that you own the house and are free to improve it on the inside and outside (with approval) of course. Generally the covenants are in place to assure home owners that nobody will do anything too radical with their property such as paint their front door pink! While this may appeal to some it might open the door to others to make even more dramatic alterations, which may not be advantageous to the majority of home owners, when it comes time for you to sell. Remember this will be an investment just as the house is from which you will be moving and guidelines are in place to help protect your investment.

Buying a home in a 55+ active adult community is similar to buying a house in any other community. You have choices of house style, elevations choices, interior features, standard upgrades and luxury upgrades. You can add on to your house with porches, decks, in-ground sprinkler systems and more, but remember you will generally have to have all of these exterior improvements approved in advance.

When you begin searching for the right active adult community you will find prices around the U.S. anywhere from less than $100,000 to well over $1.5 million for luxury, 55+ communities. The choices are many and if you begin by conducting a thorough online search you will find a community that suits your needs and most importantly your budget.

IV.   *Determining your aging senior's needs*

The very first thing that needs to be done is for you to sit down and begin asking questions of the aging senior in your life whom you believe would benefit from a new living accommodation.

It is very important to really listen to what they express regarding needs and preferences. We must remember that in most cases they are making decisions for themselves. It is our job as the children of our senior loved one to listen and support them. We must guide and help them make the best decision for themselves.

This is something you need to do before you begin your journey for a new living accommodation for your senior loved one. You have to understand your needs as well as the needs of your loved one, who may need assistance. Unless both of you get help and relief, physically and emotionally, then you may not have arrived at the best solution.

My wife and I realized quickly that her mother needed more than we were physically and emotionally able to give her for any length of time, because of our careers and we were still helping our young adult children. Additionally my wife's siblings were not in the area to offer support when it was needed in an emergency, so we were faced with the task of doing all of the research and leg work on our own. Ideally, if two or more family members can assist in the process, it will go faster, smoother and everyone will suffer less angst.

Questions you need to ask yourself as you begin the process (Assessing the needs)

- How flexible are you or your spouse with your work to be available for your loved one when he/she needs assistance? If at least one of you has the ability to take time from work, a few hours here and there each week, then you are fortunate and it will make a difference in your search for the right senior accommodations.

- In what physical condition is your loved one? (Circle a yes or no on each line)

Do they need the use of a cane or walker?	yes	no
Do they need a wheelchair?	yes	no
Do they need someone to remind them daily to take their medicine and in the proper dosage?	yes	no
Do you or someone else have to administer the medications?	yes	no
Do they have physical disabilities that prevent them from getting around easily on their own?	yes	no
Are they fearful of falling down and hurting themselves even in their own home?	yes	no

Do they need to have regular doctor visits for their conditions?	yes	no
Do they need assistance to visit their doctor?	yes	no
Are they forgetful and to what degree?	yes	no
Are you uncomfortable leaving them alone in their home/apartment for an entire day and night?	yes	no
Do they tell you they feel afraid and don't know if they can stay alone?	yes	no
Do they still drive a car?	yes	no
Should they be driving	yes	no
The question you should ask yourself is "Am I afraid to ride as a passenger in a car driven by my senior loved one?"		
Do they now cook for themselves?	yes	no
Does this make you uncomfortable?	yes	no
Are you afraid that they might burn themselves?	yes	no

Is there mostly non-nutritious food in their refrigerator?   yes   no

If you answer yes to most of these questions then you may want to begin seeking some help for your loved one in the form a new living accommodation designed for seniors. In the very least you will want to consider having an in-home care provider spend some time with your aging loved one. This will give you some time to plan for a more permanent solution if needed.

If you are still not convinced then there is one sure way for you to make the determination of whether or not your loved one requires additional care and I recommend this highly.

Recommendation:
Spend 24 hours with your aging loved one and observe their behavior. You will learn first-hand what they are doing, how they are doing it and if they are successful living completely alone anymore. Remember to conduct this exercise with an open mind and simply witness the behavior of your loved one.

V. The search for a new senior living accommodation: (They are all different)

Interim Care:

Once we determined the needs of my mother-in-law and our own needs, we began the task of searching for care. As an interim measure, because she was recovering from bronchitis, we elected to provide in-home care on an as needed basis. This turned into 24 hour care for about one week, simply to make sure she didn't fall and end up in the hospital before we had the opportunity to support a change for a new living accommodation.

It is very important for you to realize that in order to be accepted and admitted into most assisted living facilities, CCRC's or nursing homes, the prospective resident must be able to meet certain minimum physical and mental standards. If they cannot, then they may have to recover and rehabilitate somewhere else before being admitted.

One thing to keep in mind about selecting in-home care is that there are many that serve your area and you must make sure to conduct a thorough interview of the company before making a selection. Some home care services are franchises and some are independently owned.

You do not want just anyone coming into the home of your loved one to offer care. There are far too many nightmare stories about hiring home health caregivers that have ended in disappointment and tragedy.

Questions you should ask the in-home care provider

- How long have they been in business?

- Are they licensed

- Do they have liability insurance?

- What kinds of care do they perform?

- Do caregivers administer medicines if necessary?

- What kind of care will they not perform? (never assume)

- How can you know if they have provided the agreed upon care?

- Will the caregiver drive the loved one to the doctor if needed and how much extra will it cost?

- Can they be available at the last minute?

- What kind of experience do their caregivers have?

- What kind of training and certification do their caregivers have and what kind of continuing training and education does the company require?

- Do the caregivers have their own transportation or do they have to rely on public transportation? This has ramifications for you.

- Once you have had a particular caregiver and you like this person, can you request this person again or do you have to take whoever is available?

- How do they charge for their services? By the hour, by the task, by the day etc.

- Do they begin charging when the caregiver leaves their home or when they arrive at your home?

- Are there a minimum number of hours for which you will be billed for services?

- Does the rate vary by the number of hours needed for care?

- Are they willing to offer references and will they permit you to call people who have used their services?

- Are they required to have a flu vaccination each year?
- Is there a supervisor on duty at their company in case of an emergency with an assigned caregiver.

Be as selective with in-home care providers as you would with a permanent facility, even though it may be for a very short period. The care provided could make a difference between being admitted to a long-term facility or not. To learn about in-home care rates in your area, call a few local home health care agencies. You can find them in local magazines, newspapers and on line.

If you do opt for in-home care, be sure to use an agency that is licensed and insured and one that conducts thorough background checks on its employees. Given the world we live in today, background checks on caregivers is something all home healthcare agencies should do. If they don't do background checks on their caregivers then move on.

For my wife's mother, our search for a new living accommodation began by reading everything we could get our hands on, from articles in newspapers, magazines, on-line and advertisements in all of these sources.

We also called some neighbors and friends who had relatives in assisted living centers, for example, to ask for their advice and suggestions and recommendations. This proved to be one of the most helpful things we did.

Below are some steps I highly recommend as you begin your search

- Call the Office on Aging in your county government. There is a great deal of information here. They act as a clearinghouse for information. While they cannot make recommendations, they can provide raw information to assist you in your search.

- Gather a list of Assisted Living homes, CCRC'S, NORC'S, Villages, and nursing facilities in your county. You can find them at your county government offices, on the Internet, in senior magazines, and local phone directories in print and online. There are many choices, which will confuse you at first. **The key to finding the right one** is to ask yourself "is this facility going to meet our needs?"

Remember, by this point you have already conducted your needs assessment. You are now going to search for those facilities that get closest to meeting those needs. You might also ask yourself if this is "a place where I would like to live when and if I am in the same situation?"

Put yourself in the place of your loved one who needs the assistance. Understand the differences between Assisted Living, CCRC'S, Nursing Homes, Villages and NORC'S (naturally occurring retirement communities). We will define each below.

- Talk with your friends, relatives and neighbors and ask if they have any suggestions.

- Talk with your priest or pastor, accountant, lawyer and employee assistance office at your company. They may have a list of facilities for you to begin calling.

- You can also contact me by email at <u>btony@ comcast.net</u> and I can arrange to work with you or recommend the appropriate professional to help find the best appropriate living accommodation and care for your senior.

Senior Housing Options that offer assistance and care

Assisted Living:

What exactly is an Assisted Living Facility and how does it differ from a Continuing Care Retirement Community (CCRC)?

In broad terms, an assisted living facility provides housing, meals, social activities, personal care services, support services, and in some cases health care services to seniors, usually defined as adults who are 50+. There is a wide variance in the level and kinds of services, which is part of the reason we decided to publish this book.

Assisted Living facilities generally offer independent living apartments and two additional levels of care. The independent living allows the resident to live in their apartment without any assistance unless the resident requests it, for which there is usually a charge.

If a resident or the facility administrators recognize the resident may need additional help they will recommend moving them to the first level of care.

The apartments are much the same as with independent living apartments however built into the rent for this level is a certain amount of care needed for daily living activities, such as administering medications etc.

There is also a third level of accommodation for those residents who need even more care and attention and it is usually on another level of the facility.

There are 36,000 + assisted living communities in the United States today. According to the Assisted Living Federation of America (ALFA), "Assisted Living is regulated in all 50 states and state regulations generally address the mandatory services a senior living residence must provide.

All settings offer 24-hour care and supervision for those who need assistance." So when you begin your search, pay very close attention to details and ask all the questions we suggest in the book.

What is a Continuing Care Retirement Community or CCRC?

These communities comprise an entire campus of living choices from private homes and independent living apartments to assisted living apartments and even skilled nursing facilities.

The residents can age in a place without having to relocate. They provide a type of housing that caters to the residents and takes care of most of their medical needs. Facilities such as these vary greatly from pure assisted living facilities.

Common Attributes of a CCRC

A CCRC can be for profit or not-for-profit businesses and usually share the following in common:

Many require a significant upfront, one-time, entrance fee depending on the size of the apartment or residence you select. We found, in our search, that these fees range from $70,000 to $500,000 plus. The fee is usually fully refundable or partially refundable upon the resident terminating their living arrangement with the facility, but not always.

In some cases, however, it is used to fund assisted living care or skilled nursing care once the resident is not able to live independently and needs extra personal and medical services.

Some CCRC facilities also require you to have, in reserve, an amount of liquid assets equal to the amount of your entrance fee. This is needed in case you become ill and need skilled nursing care beyond that which is anticipated.

In addition to the large upfront, entrance fee, the CCRC facility charges a monthly residence fee (rent) to cover the cost of living in the facility. There are also vast differences in the amount of monthly rent to be paid which usually covers utilities.

CCRC's provide independent living accommodations for residents (apartments and suites) as well as assisted living facilities and skilled nursing facilities. They vary greatly, however in charges for services, variety of services, and proximity of the assisted living and skilled nursing facilities to the independent living residences.

These facilities are usually self-contained for the residents to be able to live out their lives at the CCRC, unlike many purely assisted living facilities. However, they require a much greater financial commitment, especially up-front. There may be tax consequences too.

Tax Consequences:
IRS Revenue Rulings: provides that residents of CCRC's may use a portion of their monthly fee and entrance fee as a personal medical deduction. The IRS does not have a published position on the correct method to use in determining that portion of your fees, which are deductible. You must discuss this matter with your personal tax advisor. There could be significant tax savings for you.

What exactly is a NORC: Naturally Occurring Retirement Community?

NORCS are another way for seniors to "age in place".

A 2010 AARP survey* found, "nearly 90 percent of people over the age of 65 want to stay in their residence for as long as possible and 80 percent believe their residence is where they will always live.

According to the survey, these baby boomers "will swell the ranks of those aged 65-plus from 34.8 million in 2000 to a projected 70.3 million in 2030, ultimately representing 20 percent of the U.S. population."

Wikipedia defines Aging in Place as "The ability to live in one's own home and community safely, independently, and comfortably, regardless of age, income, or ability level."

If one is a younger senior or a baby boomer (one born between 1946-1964) there is still time to make this decision, to save money and to plan for the 'golden years' although many may continue to work beyond the typical retirement age of 65-67.

NORC is a funny word, and I didn't make it up. On the contrary, the word is recognized by your local, state, and federal government, and has been in use since 1986. NORC is an acronym, which stands for "Naturally Occurring Retirement Community" and is an aging in place initiative.

Basically, a NORC is a place (a building, a development, a neighborhood) with a sizeable senior community that wasn't purpose-built as a senior community.

What counts as a "sizeable elderly population" varies from place to place (and from one level of government to the next), but NORCS are important because once a community meets the respective criteria, it becomes eligible for local, state, and federal funds retroactively to provide that community with the support services elderly populations typically need.

These include (but are not limited to): case management and social work services; health care management and prevention programs; education, socialization, and recreational activities; and volunteer opportunities for program participants and the community. To give you an example of how widespread these communities are, there are 27 NORCS in New York City, located in 4 boroughs.

*From an article in AARPBulletinToday, Feb. 2010

Naturally Occurring Retirement Communities is a demographic term describing neighborhoods or buildings in which a large segment of the residents are older adults.

Successful programs include the following elements and themes:

Seniors age in place (promoting independent living).

Defined geographical boundaries (as concentrated as possible).

Empowering seniors—enable them to be independent.

An environment of personal and physical security for the seniors served.

Create community—there is a connectedness among the seniors involved and between the seniors and the providers (support systems).

Partnerships that are organized or directed by a lead agency—the collaboration of service agencies results in centralized, targeted services.

Basket of services. Core services include healthcare, social work, and socialization. There are also ancillary services that are dependent on the particular needs and interests of each community.

Where the seniors live—on-site or in close proximity.

Maximizing existing services of the community, whether by avoiding duplication of services or by accessing untapped services.

Meeting unmet needs of the seniors—closing the gap of existing services.

Enhancing the quality of life of the seniors served.

Utilizing volunteerism—both intergenerational and by the seniors themselves (utilize seniors as resources).

Buy-in/commitment from the community. It is important that "the programs build in community support and local ownership from the seniors and other essential stake holders, such as building owners/operators."

The services provided to them come primarily from volunteers in the area of the seniors. Services include home repair, social activities, volunteer support, and discounts at local merchants. The individual NORC program can charge modest dues, but gets most of its funding from grants and relies extensively on volunteers.

One NORC in western St. Louis, MO has 600 members and a local university provides volunteers from the student body. There are others affiliated with universities such as LaSalle in Massachusetts.

NORCs began about 20 years ago and today number approximately 300 throughout the country. They are located in areas with heavy concentrations of seniors and are "natural" in the sense that they are not brick-and-mortar retirement complexes.

Seniors who belong to NORC's age in place in their homes. Other NORCs receive government support and provide extensive social services, which is the case in a network of more than 50 such communities in metropolitan New York. The U.S. Administration on Aging (AoA), the Federal Agency, administers Older Americans Act programs, including the National NORCs Initiative.

Sources: Information on NORCS from Norcs.org;

USNews article Oct. 7, 2009 by Philip Moeller

From an article, "Aging in Place" by Peter Wulfhorst, Posted May 13, 2013

What are Villages?

One of the most popular aging-in-place housing options for seniors today are Villages. The concept began at Beacon Hill Village in Boston in 2001. This membership organization was created by a group of Beacon Hill residents of long standing as an alternative to moving to assisted living communities or retirement communities.

According to a study by Emily A. Greenfield, Ph.D., "Villages are defined as "membership-driven, grassroots organizations run by volunteers and paid staff (to) coordinate access to affordable services . . . and offer vetted-discounted providers" *(Village to Village Network [VtV Network])*.

The Village model emphasizes the provision of supportive services (e.g., transportation, home maintenance, companionship) and referrals to existing community services. Villages are expected to be initiated and governed by the consumers they serve rather than service providers and to rely on membership dues more than government funds, grants, or fees for individual services *(McWhinney-Morse, 2009)*.

"Village and NORC program models appear to share a number of essential features, including an emphasis on promoting aging in place; serving a geographically defined service area; coordinating efforts of voluntary and formal support systems; enhancing social capital among older adults; promoting consumer engagement; and enhancing the availability, accessibility, and affordability of existing services" *(Greenfield, Scharlach, Lehning,& Davitt, 2012)*.

There are about 100 Villages operating across the country, in Canada, Australia and the Netherlands, with another 125 in development. There are eight (8) operating in the District of Columbia with Capitol Hill Village as the largest.

Kathryn (Katie) McDonough, Executive Director, of the Capitol Hill Village (CHV), one of the largest and best funded in the country said, "We are an organization of about 270 household members and 290 local volunteers in the Capitol Hill neighborhood represented by the Village." She and one other staffer as well as a board of directors oversee the coordination of services made available to members.

They offer seniors a "Care Coordination Services" program which helps seniors in the Village navigate the often times cumbersome health care system. They assign a volunteer to be a "buddy" to the senior needing care and attention during the process of getting to a care provider or hospital and making sure all of the details are handled. Katie said, "It is one of the most important and valuable services we offer."

McDonough said the CHV belongs to the VTV Network (Village to Village), an association of Villages, based in the Boston market, because they represent a valuable resource for her and the CHV. The number of Villages is growing as seniors and boomers are becoming cognizant of a current or future need to be able to continue to live in their homes as they age and need more help.

Assisted living and retirement communities such as CCRC's can be very expensive for many seniors and they still have a stigma attached as a place of no return for many seniors. According to the AARP, a vast majority of seniors would prefer to age in place in their own homes and Villages are certainly one of the most viable options that meet that need.

The Green House Project

"Long term care continues to be a challenge for many middle income seniors in the Village and across the country, said Katie McDonough.

They have assets tied up in their homes that have appreciated over decades, but they are not necessarily flush with cash. She is researching a way to help solve that problem by working with a concept called The Green House.

"The Green House model alters facility size, interior design, staffing patterns, and methods of delivering skilled professional services," according to an NCB Capital Impact article at http://www.ncbcapitalimpact.org. "This is a very real concept that could work for CHV," said Katie. Read more about the Greenhouse Project on page 46.

Aging-in-place communities allow seniors to live in their own homes and receive assistance from others in their community. A few years ago, Harry Rosenberg and his wife, Barbara Filner, met with some neighbors about starting an aging-in-place "village" in the Burning Tree community of Bethesda, Md.

The idea: "If neighbors could help one another with basic services such as transportation and simple home maintenance and with friendly visits, people could stay in their homes longer as they aged."

It took 19 months of planning and organizing, but Burning Tree Village accepted its first request for assistance in November 2008 helping an 81-year-old widow take out her trash and driving her to the doctor." You can learn more about villages by visiting, www.aarp.org. or any number of other Web sites.

Greenfield study

According to a study by Emily A. Greenfield, PhD, for the Rutgers School of Social Work, "The NORC program model has been defined, in part, as a "community-level intervention in which older adults, building owners and managers, service providers, and other community partners create a network of services and volunteer opportunities to promote aging in place. . . ." (Bedney et al., 2010, p. 304)."

Greenfield surveyed "program leaders representing 69 Villages and 63 NORC programs from January to June 2012 and results showed Village members were more likely than NORC program participants to be younger, less functionally impaired, more economically secure, and reside in higher socioeconomic communities. Also NORC programs reported offering more traditional health and social services, had more paid staff and relied more on government funding than Villages.

"The NORC program model was designed to be connected to existing housing and service organizations and emphasizes collaborations among diverse stake-holders (Vladeck, 2004). In contrast, the Village model was developed outside of the existing health and social service systems by older adults themselves and has been described as doing "anything and everything that . . . members want and need" (VtV Network, n.d.).

[1]School of Social Work, Rutgers, The State University of New Jersey, New Brunswick, New Jersey.

The Weinberg Foundation and the Greenhouse Approach

Another noteworthy program in which the Weinberg Foundation, one of the largest philanthropic organizations in the U.S., supports is known as the Greenhouse approach to residential long term care. Michael Marcus, Program Director, Older Adults, said, "There are now 120 Greenhouse projects in the U.S. with each Greenhouse residence accommodating 10 older residents."

According to the <u>Greenhouse Project</u> web site, "Each Green House home is designed to transform the institutional nursing facility into a small, residential environment. Greenhouse homes fit within the current regulatory and reimbursement structures, and are thus able to nurture people of all abilities, disabilities and financial circumstances."

The Foundation is in the process of funding a Greenhouse project in New York and has made a commitment to fund the project with $8 million this fiscal year. Marcus was enthusiastic about the Foundation's involvement in the Greenhouse approach saying it is an illustration of the "culture change project" which he believes will become a new way of life for older adults. In fact, Marcus said, "This culture change project will be the wave of the future".

In April of 2012 Maryland's first Green House residence for older adults was officially opened. The $12.6 million Green House Residences at Stadium Place is Maryland's first Green House community and was developed by the

Govans Ecumenical Development Corp., or GEDCO, and will be operated by Catholic Charities.

The Weinberg Foundation committed just over $2 million to GEDCO for the Green House Residences and is another example of Weinberg Foundation supporting the "culture change" approach to residential care of older adults.

The "Green House" Residences at Stadium Place are home to older adults who require skilled nursing or short-stay rehabilitation care.

As an alternative to a traditional nursing home, a Green House "residence" houses 10-12 people, each of whom has a private bedroom and bathroom and they are made to feel as though they are aging in place in a home-like setting.

Marcus said, "Integral to the concept is a common area known as the hearth, rather like a great room, a beautiful kitchen, and dining room."

"Older adults living in a Greenhouse residence are encouraged to participate in as many aspects of the residence as they want such as determining their activities and what meals to prepare in an effort to demonstrate their independence," said Marcus.

AARP research demonstrates that the vast majority of boomers and seniors in the U.S. want to age in place and the Greenhouse approach is a design concept that makes older residents feel as though they are at home.

In fact, Marcus said he thinks "home modification programs will become very popular" as a way for older adults to age in place in their own homes. He further added that the Foundation's initiative of lending durable medical equipment (DME) products will be a very important initiative in this effort.

Multi-Generational Housing (MGH)

When my wife was growing up her maternal grandmother lived with them for many years until she was no longer able and had to move to a nursing home. This was fairly common practice for many American families in the 60's and 70's and was and still is common practice in other cultures across the globe.

One of the major differences between that kind of multi-generational housing arrangement and one today is that homes in the 60's and 70's were not equipped to provide home features necessary for a safe, comfortable environment for the senior population in the house.

There were also no remodeling guidelines or standards for equipping a house to accommodate the needs of an aging senior. Everyone in the house just "put up with the arrangement" which was not always easy and created great frustration for everyone under that roof.

The Pew Research Center produced a Social and Demographic Trends Report in March 2010. It summarizes how there is "a revival of a practice of multi-generational housing since 1980." Their information was based on Census data and their own public opinion survey data.

"The multi-generational American family household is staging a comeback-driven in part by the job losses and home foreclosures of recent years but, more so by demographic changes that have been gathering steam for decades."

Some highlights of the report show:

"In 2008, an estimated 49 million Americans, or 16% of the total U.S. population, lived in a family household that contained at least two adult generations or a grandparent and at least one other generation. In 1980, this figure was just 28 million, or 12% of the population."

"This 33% increase since 1980 in the share of all Americans living in such households represents a sharp trend reversal, according to the study."

"The growth since 1980 in these multi-generational households is partly the result of demographic and cultural shifts, including the rising share of immigrants in the population and the rising median age of first marriage of all adults.

An estimated 51.5 million people live in multi-generational housing, which typically means three generations under one roof. That number is expected to increase as baby boomers get older. At least 10,000 Americans will turn 65 each day for the next 19 years, according to the Pew Research Center.

Whether to take care of elderly parents or just to create efficiencies for young couples and parents, more families are moving in together. The Williams family is a case in point.

When Art Williams' mother was injured in a work accident, he and his wife decided to have her move in with them. While he was happy to take care of his mom, and she was happy to take care of his two young children while he and his wife worked, the arrangement was a crowded one.

"It was our first time living with someone else, and it was definitely different," says Williams, 33. "When she first moved in, my son was four or five, and he kept asking when Grandma was going to go home."

But last September, Williams found a solution that made his entire family-even his young son-happy. He bought a NextGen home from Lennar, a national builder that offers multi-generational housing in the Los Angeles area.

"The concept is to create a home-within-a-home," says Jeff Roos, a Lennar regional president. "You have a full home with a separate, private apartment attached to it."

NextGen homes look like any other, but each includes a separate "near" apartment, featuring a bedroom, bathroom, living area and kitchenette. It is "near" rather than "full" because it lacks a stove, which would technically turn the separate space into a new residence in most zoning codes. The apartment even has its own entrance.

The idea was born out of a trend that took hold during the recession, where families doubled up to save on housing costs. Kids who had run out of money moved back into childhood homes, heads of families who had lost their homes to foreclosure moved in with siblings, or mom and dad settled in with their children's families.

"When that occurred, people lived in a guest bedroom, sometimes a dual master suite, but they didn't have an independent living space where they can hang out, cook, watch TV, play games, do their laundry," Roos says. "They're not just living together; they're living on top of each other."

Roos' concept isn't entirely new. The American Institute of Architects has been tracking the popularity of separate living space for years.

"There was a term called 'accessory apartments' that dates back quite a while," says Kermit Baker, chief economist for the AIA. "I think it was a popular concept 20 to 25 years ago that expanded out to au pair or in-law suites."

The trend wound down over the years, but it picked up speed again when the economy took a nosedive. In the AIA's most recent annual survey of architects, 26.7 percent said the design concept was on the rise.

"It's something that's on the radar screen for designers," Baker says. "But I wouldn't say it's blasting off in popularity. Instead, there's a clear niche for this."

Lennar has tapped that niche and has found success across the country with its NextGen designs. The company first rolled out the homes in Phoenix in 2011, and it has since extended the concept to 120 communities in 10 states. Lennar is betting that demand will continue to increase.

"This is a product that is not just a recession buster," Roos says. "It has the ability to change some lifestyles for a long period of time."

Their NextGen home certainly changed the lifestyle of the Williams family. Williams' mother spends her days with the family in the main house, but the three generations separate at night and get much-needed alone time. They can now choose how to spend their weekends: as a group or on their own.

"For us, it wasn't that we couldn't have lived all together, but this is so much better," Williams says

"But at a time of high unemployment and a rising foreclosures, the number of households in which multiple generations of the same family double up under the same roof has spiked significantly. Our report finds that from 2007 to 2008, the number of Americans living in a multi-generational family household grew by 2.6 million."

"This trend has affected adults of all ages, especially the elderly and the young. For example, about one in five adults, ages 25 to 34 now live in a multi-generational household and so do one-in-five adults ages 65 and older."

If you are considering having your parent(s) or other aging senior live in your house with you and perhaps your children, because you genuinely care about them and their well-being and you believe it is the best alternative housing accommodation than anything else you have researched, then perhaps you should consider creating a multi-generational household. If this is the case there are some serious questions you should ask yourself such as:

Has your home been modified for your senior's needs?

Do you need to make any renovations or are you planning to move into an already modified home?

Does your home have a bedroom, bathroom, kitchen and laundry room all on the main floor?

If you are going to buy one that has been modified does it allow your senior to live on the ground level.

Does your home or one you will buy have wide doorways?

Does the home have stairs at the entranceway? (This will be problematic)

Does the senior's bathroom have a walk-in shower with a built-in bench?

Does the shower head pull down and is it adjustable?

Does the home have non-slippery floor surfaces?

Does the home have lower cabinets for easy access by the senior?

Does your home have faucets and fixtures that are easy to turn?

Are the doorknobs easy to turn?

Are there grab bars installed?

Answering these questions will be critical before making a decision to convert your house into a multi-generational house to accommodate an aging senior.

Boomers don't usually want to think about these things because they don't want to admit that they are getting older and in fact may need to modify their home at some point even if they are not having a senior move in just yet creating a multi-generational house.

To have a proper functioning, safe, comfortable home for you and your senior(s) then you will need to make modifications or move to a previously modified house. Either way it could be a big expense.

Sharon Graham Neiderhaus completed her master's thesis at Stanford on multigenerational living, which has since been published in a book_on the topic. Neiderhaus reveals that "the number of Americans that live in multigenerational homes has grown 40% since 1990 but the shift is not exclusively a rising immigrant population."

A 2010 Pew poll states that "nearly 50 million Americans currently live in a multigenerational home and the number is expected to rise in coming years, making the multigenerational housing trend less of a trend and more of a market reality."

According to Immersion Active, a seniors marketing company, "seniors and their caregivers spent $25B in aging-in-place remodeling projects in 2012" and spending for aging-in-place assistive technology will dramatically increase by 2025.

Sources:

Pew Research Center's Trends Report, March 2010

"All in The Family", a book by Sharon Graham Neiderhaus

Immersion Active

2013 CBS Interactive Inc./Money Watch/June 17, 2013/Housing Trends Article

Nursing Homes or Nursing Facilities

These facilities offer 24-hour a day care for those who can no longer live independently. Nursing homes are equipped with medical professionals and supplies to offer specialized care for those with severe illnesses or injuries.

Trained staff members assist residents with personal and daily activities such as getting out of bed, bathing, eating, using the bathroom and regulating medications.

Typically nursing home facilities offer daily meal plans, laundry, housekeeping, medical services and a wide array of planned recreational activities.

Nursing homes can vary greatly and unfortunately there is a great deal of fear associated with nursing homes today and when you have toured as many as my wife and I have, you will begin to understand why this is so.

While there are some nursing homes we would never consider as a residence for our seniors, there are some very fine ones as well. Your job is to understand which one is best suited for your senior.

The following information is important for you to know as you explore your options for additional care for your senior. The emotional state of your senior is crucial to your success in finding a suitable living accommodation, which is why you need to be as informed as possible before you begin your journey.

J. Anthony Burke

"Seniors Fear Loss of Independence, Nursing Homes MoreThan Death"

"Senior citizens fear moving into a nursing home and losing their independence more than they fear death, according to a study, "Aging in Place in America," commissioned by Clarity and The EAR Foundation, which also found that the Baby Boomer children of seniors also fear for their parents.

Boomers express particular concern about their parents' emotional and physical wellbeing should they have to enter a nursing home, finds the study, which examines the attitudes and anxieties of the nation's elderly population (via MediaPost). When asked what they fear most, seniors rated loss of independence (26%) and moving out of home into a nursing home (13%) as their greatest fears. Death was cited as the greatest fear for just 3% of seniors."

Excerpt from an article published in Marketing Charts on 01/08/09
© 2007-2009 Watershed Publishing LLC and Media Buyer Planner LLC

The Actual Search for Assisted Living or other senior living accommodation:

The first steps in the search will be to:

1. Phone the facility or community for an appointment to take a tour and to meet with an administrator and or marketing representative. You should plan on spending about 2 hours with the representative at this first meeting.

    That is about average in our experience, because it involves a tour of the entire facility, including rooms, dining area, common areas for residents and a meeting with the administrator.

    Be prepared to ask questions, lots of questions at these initial meetings and don't assume anything. We will give you a list of suggested questions in the next chapter.

2. Get all the printed information from each facility that they will provide.

3. Observe the residents and the staff as you walk through the facility and notice how they interact with each other. Make special note of how the staff talks with the residents.

    *   Are they patient?

    *   Do they explain things carefully and fully?

- Do they give the residents their full attention?

- Are the residents smiling and do they appear to enjoy living there?

Talk with some of the residents and ask them how they like living there. Ask them to tell you what they like and don't like. You will learn a great deal this way.

If the administrator suggests it is not necessary for you to talk with any residents, politely thank them and move on to another community. Ask yourself, "What are they afraid of?"

4. Ask if you can have breakfast, lunch or dinner in their dining room. You may want to do this to determine for yourself the quality and quantity of the food and the level of service. Many facilities will agree and usually offer you the meal at no cost.

5. Observe how they maintain the facility, including the common living areas and rooms. Look for whether the floors, carpet, and units are clean. Don't be afraid to comment on areas that concern you.

   Remember you want assurance that your loved one will be living in a facility that cares about the health and cleanliness of their building as well as the health of the residents. They go hand-in-hand.

6. We recommend you visit at least 4-5 facilities, because you will find variances in type of care, size

of rooms, quality of staff and food and prices for accommodations and care.

7. After you have visited the facilities, take the materials home and review them again as soon as possible so that the information is fresh in your mind and you can make some notes for the next step, which is meeting with your loved one to review the choices.

You may have to make some initial decisions beforehand and narrow down the list of choices for your loved one to make the process go more smoothly. To ask your elderly relative to travel to 4 or 5 facilities and spend 2 hours at each plus travel time, may be too much to ask and too much to expect of them.

8. Meet with your loved one to review your choices of facilities and be prepared to tell him or her what you like about them, why you like them and why they would be good for them.

Then proceed to get agreement on which ones you will visit together. Make the second appointments and take your loved one on each of them or as many as they physically can attend.

9. After these second appointments, be prepared to discuss the pros and cons with your loved one and narrow down the choices to one. You will end up going back to this facility again to make sure you are comfortable with the choice and to meet with the facility nurse for a medical evaluation.

This is important so that they can make a recommendation for how much, if any, initial care your loved one will need in order to become as independent as quickly as possible within the facility.

VI. The Finances

After you have successfully determined the needs of your loved one and your needs, then it is time to get a firm handle on their finances.

This is a very important step before you begin to search for any assistance, because there are many types of senior accommodations and they are all priced differently. Finding the one that is affordable for you and that meets your other needs is going to be important, so understanding what shape your loved one's finances are in is critical at this stage.

When you finally decide on an accommodation such as an assisted living facility, a CCRC, a NORC, a nursing home, having them age in place, or move into your house, you will need to have all finances, including Power of Attorney, Will and Living Will in order.

The facility will generally require copies of each legal document. Some may not ask for a copy of the Will, but most will require a copy of the other documents.

Pre-Questions:
Before you begin what may be perceived as an "inquisition" by your loved one, you might want to lay the groundwork for why you are inquiring about their finances. If they know you have their best interest at heart they will be more apt to cooperate with you and you definitely need their cooperation.

Now some questions:

- What is your loved one's monthly income? When do the checks arrive each month?
- Are the checks deposited into their checking or savings account or sent to their home?
- Which bank(s) or credit union(s) holds their accounts?
- What are the components and sources of this income?
  - Pension
  - Social Security
  - Investment income
  - Bonds
  - Stock dividends
  - CD interest
  - Trust income
  - Proceeds from sale of real estate
  - Other income

It is important for you to make a list of each component of income for your loved one, along with expiration date of CD's etc. so that you can help him or her prepare financially for paying for their care.

We recommend creating a chart listing each source of income with address, telephone number and contact person at each financial source. This way you or your loved one will be able to quickly notify them of any change in your loved one's condition, address etc.

What is a durable power of attorney?

A Durable Power of Attorney is a legal document that insures that someone you trust will be available to handle the financial tasks that arise if one becomes incapacitated.

Bills need to be paid, bank deposits need to be made and someone will have to handle benefits and insurance paperwork. A Durable Power of Attorney may be the best way for you to handle all of these tasks. You should consult your attorney to have them draw up a "Durable Power of Attorney" for your loved one and yourself while you are at it!

What is a Living Will?

Living Wills help medical staff and others to make decisions about an individual's care and treatment if one becomes seriously ill and not able to speak for him or herself.

Basically a Living Will is a document that states how we wish to be treated if we become incapacitated by illness, injury or old age. The Living Will is designed to provide explicit direction in near-death situations-specifying whether the patient wants all possible medical intervention or certain limits on treatment.

Remember a Living Will deals with health issues. You should consult your attorney to have them draw up a Living Will for your loved one and yourself while you are at it!

What about Long Term Care Insurance?

Long-term care insurance (**LTC** or **LTCI**), is an insurance product sold in the United States and United Kingdom and helps provide for the cost of long-term care beyond a predetermined period. Long-term care insurance covers care generally not covered by health insurance, Medicare, or Medicaid.

People who require long-term care are generally not sick in the traditional sense, but instead, are unable to perform the basic activities of daily living (ADLs) such as dressing, bathing, eating, toileting, continence, transferring (getting in and out of a bed or chair), and walking.

According to the American Association for Long Term Care Insurance, "Tax-qualified LTCI premiums are considered a medical expense. For an individual who itemizes tax deductions, medical expenses are deductible to the extent that they exceed the current amount required to meet the individual's Adjusted Gross Income (AGI).

The amount of the LTCI premium treated as a medical expense is limited to the eligible LTCI premiums, as defined by Internal Revenue Code 213(d), based on the age of the insured individual. That portion of the LTCI premium that exceeds the eligible LTCI premium is not included as a medical expense.

Individual taxpayers can treat premiums paid for tax-qualified long-term care insurance for themselves, their spouse or any tax dependents (such as parents) as a personal medical expense. Please consult your tax attorney or CPA to see if you qualify for a tax deduction.

According to the AALTCI, age is not a determining factor in requiring long-term care. Nearly 60 percent of individuals over age 65 will require at least some type of long-term care services during their lifetime. About 40% of those receiving long-term care today are between 18 and 64. Remember that once a change of health occurs, long-term care insurance may not be available.

In the United States, Medicaid provides some of the benefits of long term care insurance. A welfare program, Medicaid does provide medically necessary services for people with limited resources who need nursing home care.

However, Medicaid generally does not cover long-term care provided in a home setting or for assisted living. People who need long-term care often prefer care in the home or in a private room in an assisted living facility.

For additional information on long term care insurance, such as types of policies, contact your insurance agent, accountant or tax attorney.

Sources:
American Association for Long Term Care Insurance (AALTCI)

VII. Be Prepared for Paperwork (and communicate with your loved one and his or her doctors)

Be prepared to fill out lots of paperwork before you finally sign the rental agreement with the facility admitting your loved one.

Also be prepared to spend many hours with your loved one taking them to doctors' appointments getting the necessary checkups, TB test and chest x-ray that all facilities require.

Essentially your loved one needs a clean bill of health before he or she can move into an Assisted Living Facility, CCRC or nursing home.

Examples of forms that will have to be filled out prior to moving in:

- Pre-move-in physical assessment filled out by your senior's primary care physician or their Nurse Practitioner.

- Resident nurse's profile; filled out by the facility nurse prior to moving in. This must be done with your loved one in attendance and is usually done at the second appointment.

- Resident profile, which gives information on your loved one's favorite activities, both recreation and religious, special foods they like and or need, their best friends names and numbers, what time they usually get up and go to bed at night, whether or not they have any sleep disturbances etc.

- Resident Funds held in Trust form (some require this so that the facility can know what monies your loved one has in trust)

- Pharmacy resident agreement . . . this form simply will instruct their pharmacy on what medications your loved one is taking and how often.

More Forms

- Physicians Report by your loved one's physician giving information on special diets, any current diagnosis of your loved one's results of TB test and more.

- Resident application will need to be filled out prior to the move in. This gives the facility information on whom to call as a contact; their current living situation, marital status, etc.

- Be prepared to give the facility a copy of your senior's social security card, medical insurance card and Medicare Card, Durable Power of Attorney and Living Will.

- Emergency Information Form. This form is sometimes needed by the facility to be able to contact another responsible party in case of an emergency, physical and or financial.

- Authorization to Release Confidential Information. This form gives the facility the authority to get medical and financial information, for example, when they need it. This will help facilitate the transmission of the information so that you or your loved one does not have to arrange for it on your own.

- Resident Rights and Grievance Procedure Acknowledgment form. This form, usually a State mandated set of rights, simply acknowledges that you and your loved one have read the facilities' residents rights information and know the process for filing a grievance when necessary.

- Resident Agreement. This is simply a rental agreement outlining the terms, conditions and costs of becoming a resident of the facility.

VIII. Questions You Must Ask the Assisted Living facility (don't assume anything)

During all of your visits to each of the facilities, you will want to take a pad of paper and pencil or pen, because you will be asking them many questions.

We found out that if you don't ask a question, the Administrator will not always volunteer the information and you could end up getting an unpleasant surprise down the road when it is too late.

It is imperative to ask the following questions of the Administrator at the facility

- How long has the facility been operating and what is the ratio of care-giving staff to residents? (for comparison purposes)

- How old is the building and does it meet fire codes? Does the facility have sprinklers in each room and in common areas?

- Will they give you a list of residents and their family member caregivers to speak with so you can find out their satisfaction level?

- How do they define their base level of care?

- What is the next level of care above the base level?

- Is there a third level of care if my loved one becomes less able to care for himself or herself? Most facilities offer three levels of care with the bottom level offering monitored care where the resident is independent, but the staff is monitoring their behavior.

The second level offers additional help for the resident in terms of helping them bathe, escorting them to meals, laundry service etc.

A third level of care is often offered where the facility staff basically offers complete care for the resident, short of lifting them in and out of bed, which they will not do. This requires special care, which may require the services of a nursing home or an interim caregiver to provide additional care at the facility.

More Questions

- Is housekeeping included in their base level of care and how much housekeeping is included and how often do they do the housekeeping?

- Do they provide laundry services with the monthly fee?

- Do they provide a laundry room on each floor for residents' use?

- Is there a cost for the resident to use the laundry?

- Are utilities included in the base rent?

- Are there any utilities such as phone and or cable included and how are they invoiced?

- What recreational, social, educational and religious activities does the facility provide?

- What daily transportation does the facility provide and do they help the resident get into and out of the vehicle?

- Do they provide religious services at the facility and or do they provide transportation to local churches and how often?

- Are there regularly scheduled and supervised shopping trips and does this cost extra?

- Does the facility provide a place for large gatherings of family and friends for parties, etc.?

- Is there catering available for these gatherings if desired?

- Do they offer supervised exercise programs for residents?

- Are there daily wellness visits provided by the facility nurse?

- Do they make daily status checks on the residents?

- Is there a full time RN on duty and for 24 hours and how many?

- Do they make provisions for special meals for residents with diets prescribed by a physician or other dietary specialists?

- Do they automatically provide as part of the base rate, medication monitoring, or is it a paid extra? Some residents, who are forgetful, will need to have their medications monitored and in some cases administered by a RN.

- If the resident is allowed to self-medicate, will they be required to lock up their medications in their room or apartment? (This issue can be traumatic to an elderly resident who may find it difficult to lock and unlock a cabinet each time he or she has to take medications).

- What amenities does the facility provide to the residents? For example, do they have a beauty shop, bank, theatre, arts and crafts room, exercise room, and game room on premises? This provides a great convenience to the residents, especially if they have difficulty getting around.

- Can the resident have small appliances in their apartment, such as a microwave, coffee maker etc.?

- Will the facility allow the resident to self-medicate (if resident is capable) or do they insist on providing medication administration management for the resident?

- Will they automatically charge extra for the medication management?

- Do they offer Alzheimer's and Dementia Care programs?

- What type of rooms do they offer? This is going to be one the most critical aspects of your decision, we have found. Your loved one will likely be moving from complete independent living in a house or a larger apartment and they may expect to have as much room in the new facility as they had been enjoying. It is imperative for you to get them to understand as soon as possible that this will not be the case.

  Most of the facilities we visited had a variety of accommodations available ranging from an efficiency to a small one bedroom apartment to shared suites and shared large rooms. Remember these shared rooms and suites share a bathroom as well.

We will say again that this will be one of the biggest issues and hurdles you will have to get over, in our experience, and one that the new resident, your loved one, will take the longest time with which to get comfortable.

It is a very sensitive issue and a big concern to the resident, because he or she will feel as if you are taking away more and more of their independent life including the special rooms and favorite furniture they have enjoyed for many years.

You need to know that many facilities will try to encourage you to move your loved one into a shared room, because of the lower cost, but mainly because the individual rooms (apartments or individual suites) are in highest demand).

- Do they provide basic furniture or do you have to bring your own?

- Are you allowed to bring your own furniture and any restrictions?

- Does the facility allow a family member to stay as a guest overnight in the resident's apartment or in a different room designated as such?

- Do they allow couples?

- What happens if one member of the couple becomes ill and needs additional care?

- Will your loved one continue to see his or her regular physician after they move in?

- Do they provide medical services such as dental and podiatry for residents and at what cost?

- Do residents have access to barbers, beauticians, and other grooming services, including hair washing, manicures, etc.

- What types of activities are available for residents, including games, movies, crafts, classes, field trips, etc.?

- Is there a social worker on community staff or as a consultant to help with the adjustment process and provide community and financial resource information?

- Do residents have the opportunity to attend religious services and visit with clergy of their respective faiths?

- Do they allow pets and is there an additional cost?

- How much will living at the facility cost each month?

- Exactly what will the extra care cost? And exactly what extra care do you provide?

- How much do I have to put down as a deposit on my new apartment and is it refundable if I change my mind?

- How much is the community fee? There is usually an up-front fee that most facilities tell you will go toward upkeep of the common areas.

  The community fees will vary however. In our search, we found a range of between $500 and $6,000. So make sure you ask and understand this fee. This fee is usually, but not always, refundable on a pro rata basis for the first 90 days after you move in. After that it will usually not be refunded.

- Is there a first and last month's deposit required at lease signing? Some facilities require it and some don't. Knowing this up-front will save you some angst.

- Does the information in the marketing brochure match the information in the resident's contract? (You must read the contract thoroughly to ensure it covers all services that the marketing people told you are part of your program. Go over every detail with a trusted friend, relative and or attorney if it will make you feel more comfortable).

- When does the facility bill for the month?

- Do they include all charges on one bill?

- When does the bill have to be paid?

- What happens if payment is late?
-
- What happens if your loved one has to go to the hospital because of illness or injury? Does the facility hold the room?

- What happens if your loved one runs out of money and can no longer afford to live there? T

  This is a critical question and one that needs to be asked and answered. Your loved one could surprise you and live to be 100, but run out of assets before that and be in deteriorating health, but not necessarily in need of a nursing home.

  Knowing what your options are now could be very important. One solution may be to apply for the Medicaid waiver program. In Maryland, it is known as the Medicaid Home and Community Based Services Waiver for Older Adults. It may be called something else in other states.

- Does your facility subscribe to the Medicaid waiver program? The waiver allows services that are typically covered by Medicaid only in a nursing facility, to be provided to eligible persons in their own homes or in assisted living facilities

This is a relatively new government subsidized program for elderly, low-income residents of assisted home facilities and believe it or not, many administrators at the facilities don't know enough about it. Find out in your state if the program exists by calling you county or state Office on Aging.

It does exist in the state of Maryland, where we live, but many assisted living homes we contacted do not subscribe. The waiver provides services to a specified maximum number of residents in the state (it will rise over the next couple of years). In order to qualify, the resident must be receiving services in Senior Assisted Housing that are certified by Department of Aging.

In Maryland, the resident must be at least 50 years old; they must be eligible for Department of Aging housing subsidies and for Medicare. There is a limit as to their monthly income and their total assets to qualify as well and they must qualify for <u>nursing facility level</u> of care to qualify. The requirements may be different in your state, so please check with your local Office on Aging.*

Source: * In Maryland check out these Web sites.
Office on Aging in Howard County Maryland <u>www.co.ho.md.us/oa/cs_office**aging**.htm</u>
Maryland Department of Aging www.mdoa.state.**md**.us

IX. *Making the decision*

After you have asked all the questions you and your loved ones consider important and you are comfortable with the costs and level of care provided by the facility, you are now ready to make the decision.

This may seem like the easiest part of the process, but in fact it may be very difficult. For us, it meant sitting down with my wife and her mother and re-examining the entire process once more. Her mother wanted to make it known that she thought she could get her strength back and she would be as healthy as she ever was and therefore may not have to move.

She very much loved her apartment and the friends she had made while living there and did not want to give all that up. While my wife and I wanted to believe this was possible, we knew from taking care of her and observing her for two months that this didn't appear to be realistic.

What we did hope was that she gained a routine, ate better, more regular meals and had care when she needed it at the assisted living facility. With this she would gain a new level of health and strength and allow her to regain a certain measure of independence, which she very much wanted.

Remember that for this to truly work and work well, you must try and get your loved one to make the decision with you so that he or she takes some ownership of the decision.

We talked with my wife's mother for a couple of weeks, before she actually signed the lease, just to make sure she felt comfortable with moving into the assisted living facility. Once the decision is made, it is time to arrange for the lease signing date and the move in date.

X.   *Arranging for the move*

If your loved one is like ours, he or she will want to have control of the process and will want to be involved in the pre-move process. There is a great deal to be accomplished as with any move.

This kind of move is especially challenging, because of the heightened emotions involved with everyone. Your loved one is going to want to be as protective of his or her personal belongings as possible, knowing full well that the space into which he or she will be moving will be much smaller.

You, on the other hand, will be trying to balance your loved one's feelings with the reality of the need to either sell, give to relatives or to charity those items that cannot be moved due to space limitations.

This is a very critical time, because you will want to be as sensitive as possible yet firm in just the right way to accomplish the task of preparing for the move.

There are things you will want to remember to do. Please keep in mind that your loved one may say he or she will make some of the phone calls, but may end up asking you to do them, because often people in their 80's or older will not want to be on hold for 5 minutes taking instructions from a computer generated voice.

Since we have had this experience with both my mother-in-law and my own mother there has been an explosion of senior care service businesses ready and able to help with virtually any aspect of senior care.

Some of the senior services are offered by downsizing specialists; senior mobility specialists (to assess and install features in the home to allow the senior to stay mobile); home management care providers; traditional caregivers; non-traditional caregivers; home modification specialists; reverse mortgage specialists, senior moving specialists; home estate auction specialists and more. There are even senior care companies that do virtually everything.

The important thing to remember is to find a service provider that has the experience in the service(s) you need, a good reputation in their industry and can be trusted.

My wife and I found it important to check and double-check all the details after my wife's mother accomplished a task, just to make sure nothing was missed.

Regardless of whether the move is from an apartment or a house, these are the things you will want to remember to do:

- Call all utilities, phone, gas and electric company, cable company, Internet Service Provider, etc. to notify of change of address.

- Arrange with the local phone provider to have a new phone number installed at the new address and make sure it is installed at least the day before the move in day so you will have phone service on move-in day if needed. You will also need to coordinate this with the facility.

- Notify publications to which he or she subscribes, that there will be a change of address.

  Send in a Postal Change of address card, which you can get at any post office branch or you can accomplish this online at http://moversguide.usps.com/

- Inventory all personal items in the house, from clothing to furniture to personal care items.

- Determine which items will be moved and which your loved one decides to leave behind.

- Get the pick up and or delivery schedule from the charities to which you will be donating.

- Arrange with a moving company or determine how you are going to do the moving as a family. Call for a rental truck or van at least 1 week in advance. Certain size trucks go fast and may not be available if you don't give enough lead-time.

- Make sure to give 30 days written notice to the property manager, if you are in an apartment complex. The landlord in the lease usually requires this.

- If you are selling your house or renting it, allow enough time to dispose of the property before you make the move and make sure to coordinate the move with the settlement date if selling or arrange for a lease back if the new Assisted Living Facility room will not be available when you need it.

- One other senior care professional that is coming onto the scene is a real estate senior specialist. There is only one that I know of in the Maryland market, at this writing, who works for a very large real estate agency and heads a division dealing with seniors and their families.

Some of the services they provide include pulling together a variety of senior care service providers to save the home owner significant time. They offer advice on how to prepare your home for sale given the sensitive nature of the move involving a senior who may also not be well.

They can also arrange for an existing home to be modified in order for the senior to age in place if that is what is needed. If this interests you reach out to me at btony@comcast.net and I will provide a referral.

XI. The Actual Move

When it is moving day to the Assisted Living Facility, you will need to get timing down. Usually, before the facility managers allow your loved one to move in, they will ask you to come in on the morning of the move-in day and sign the lease for the new apartment or room.

You will get the keys, turn over copies of the Living Will and the Durable Power of Attorney etc. These are all formalities, which must be done before you can move the furniture and the resident into the facility.

You will want to ask the Facility Administrator with whom you have been working, if you have to arrange for a designated move-in time. This is always desirable since you will actually have a block of time reserved to use the loading dock at the facility and not have to wait in line for your turn.

If they do not reserve times you will have to get to the loading dock of the new facility and take your chances. When we did this, there were two families doing the same thing and they were ahead of us at the loading dock.

Since we did not want to wait (which could have been a couple of hours) we decided to park the van away from the loading dock and walk a little further. This is not meant to scare you but is something about which you need to be aware.

Once you get moved into the facility, the apartment is yours and you will want to get acclimated as soon as possible so that your loved one begins to feel at home.

We found that getting furniture and personal items in place and pictures, curtains hung etc. is vital, since his or her life has just been uprooted dramatically.

Your goal should be to work with your loved one to make sure that everything is where it should be and not leave it up to them to do it. Your loved one will be a much happier, healthier, well-adjusted resident once everything is in place.

The faster you can make it happen, the quicker your life will return to normal as well. Even if you live close by, consider having someone stay with your loved one in their new home for the day and even for the night. This will make a big difference in allowing your loved one to become acclimated faster.

References

Greenfield, E. A., Scharlach, A., Lehning, A., & Davitt, J. (2012). A conceptual framework for examining the promise of the NORC Program and Village models to promote aging in place. *Journal of Aging Studies, 26*, 273-284. doi:10.1016/j.jaging.2012.01.003

Vladeck, F. (2004). *A good place to grow old: New York's model for NORC supportive service programs*. New York: United Hospital Fund.

McWhinney-Morse, S. (2009). Beacon hill village. *Generations, 33*, 85-86.

"Social & Demographic Trends Project." Pew Research Center*, Washington, D.C. March 18, 2010, accessed on line June 2013

XII. Follow Up and Special Thought

Remember if you are a "boomer" and member of the "sandwich generation" or a senior, you do not need to face these challenges alone.

Please know that we are there to support each other and my wife and I are there to help you should you need it. You can email me at btony@comcast.net or offer questions and comments on my blog at http://www.boomersandseniors.wordpress.com.

My wife and I wish you the very best as you prepare for this journey of moving a loved one from the normalcy of their life to something that will, appear at first, to be life threatening.

If you know how to begin the process and ask all the right questions during your search, get organized and allow enough time to accomplish all that has to be done, you and your loved one will be much happier as a result.

You will definitely save substantial time, money and angst in the process as we did. We probably saved my mother-in-law thousands of dollars in expenses as a result of our research. Your loved one might even thank you for all your time, care and love.

I hope we have given you some useful suggestions and help with this book and believe if you follow what we have suggested, you will save yourself and your loved one a great deal of anxiety during this trying time. Our very best to you . . .

One last thought . . .

When you have a loved one
Approaching their senior years,
You notice changes in how they move,
They stay at home a lot more
Begin to shuffle along the floor
Believe they still have more to prove

They've worked very hard, struggled at times
Providing support for family and others,
Learned from mistakes, we now view them as wise
For what would they wish, given their druthers?

Some may wish again to be young,
Others like status that comes with age
Most believe there are battles to be won
Some as small as just walking, turning a page!

We need to understand that we can do more
To help them in their time of need
A kind word, a smile, a helping hand with the door
And don't expect a reward for the deed

Offer to help, it's not that hard, just try
Make an effort, you'll feel good, you see
Life goes by fast, in the blink of an eye,
You may one day say, "That could be me!"